STEM!

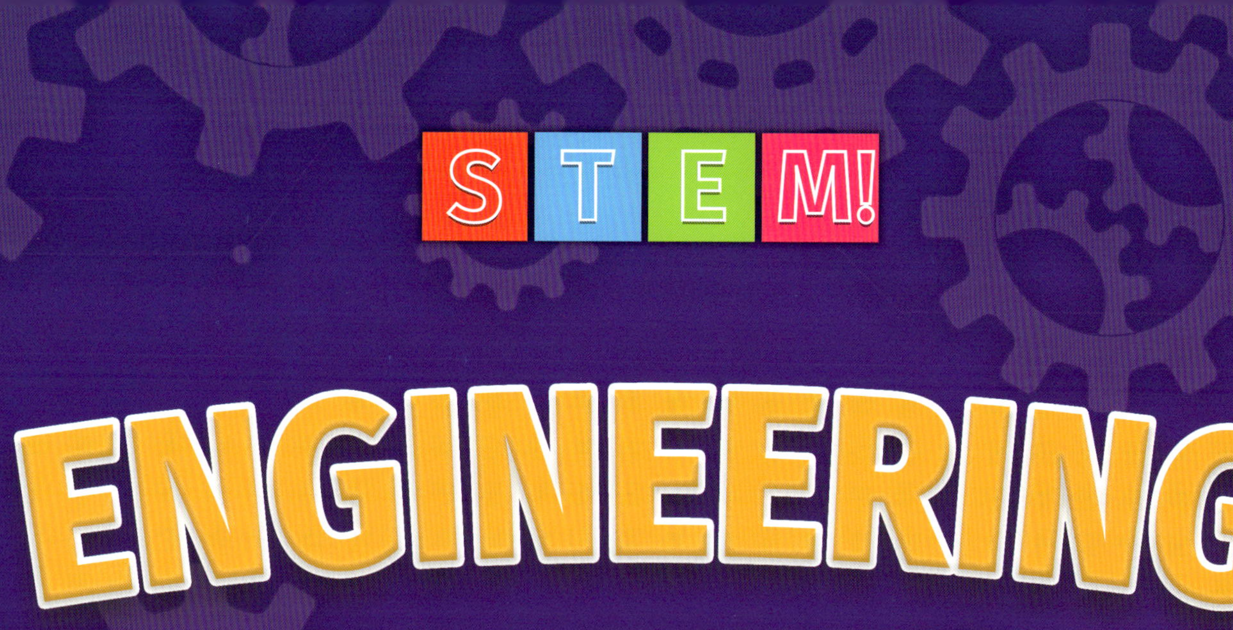

ENGINEERING

EDITED BY
MARZIA TEMPOLI

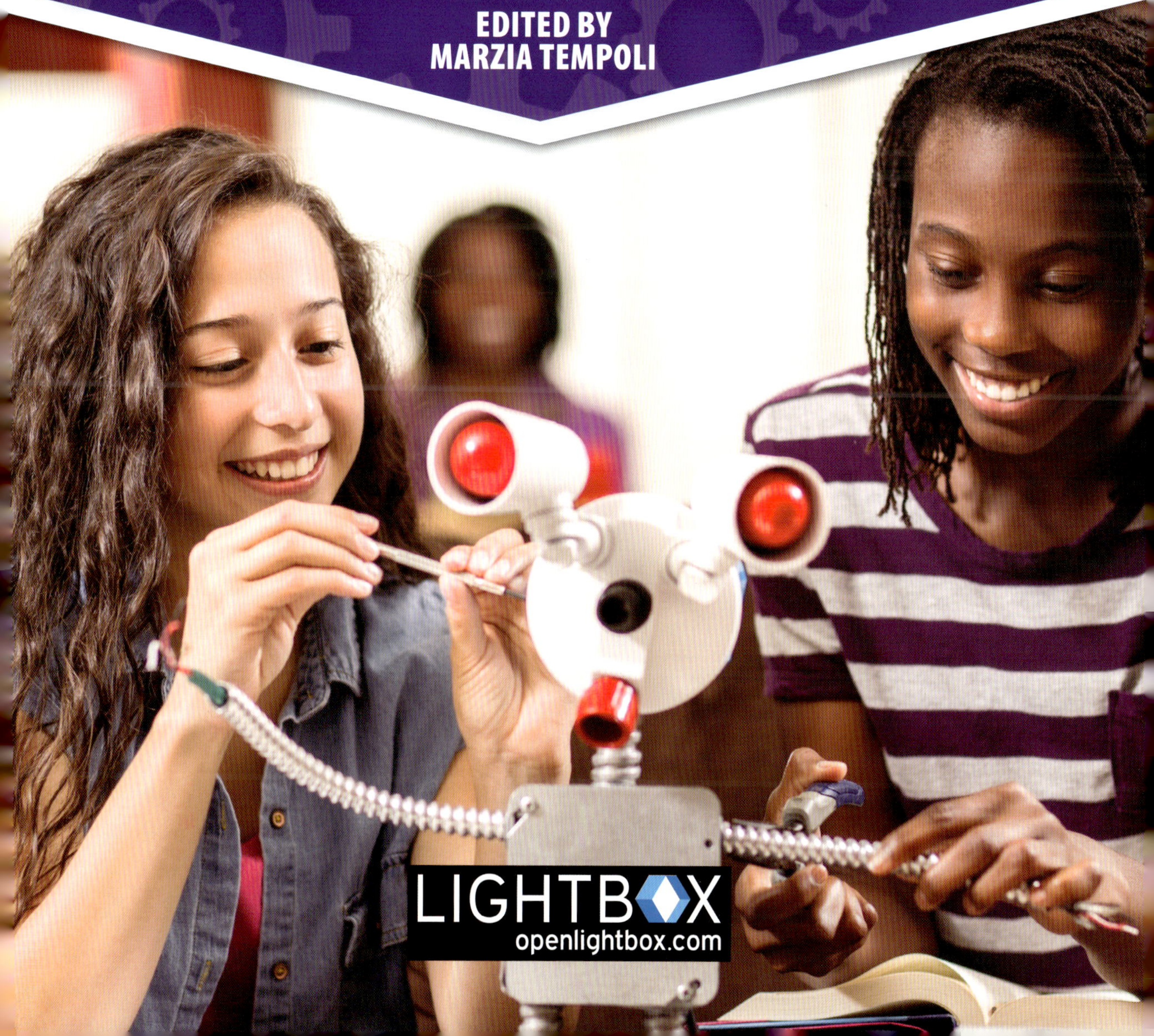

LIGHTBOX
openlightbox.com

LIGHTBOX

Go to **www.openlightbox.com** and enter this book's unique code.

ACCESS CODE

LBXA4837

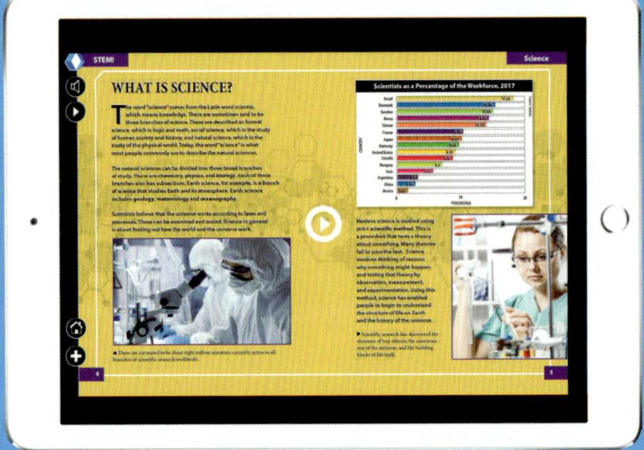

Lightbox is an all-inclusive digital solution for the teaching and learning of curriculum topics in an original, groundbreaking way. Lightbox is based on National Curriculum Standards.

STANDARD FEATURES OF LIGHTBOX

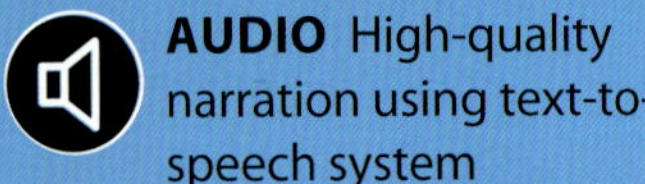

AUDIO High-quality narration using text-to-speech system

ACTIVITIES Printable PDFs that can be emailed and graded

SLIDESHOWS Pictorial overviews of key concepts

VIDEOS Embedded high-definition video clips

WEBLINKS Curated links to external, child-safe resources

TRANSPARENCIES Step-by-step layering of maps, diagrams, charts, and timelines

INTERACTIVE MAPS Interactive maps and aerial satellite imagery

QUIZZES Ten multiple choice questions that are automatically graded and emailed for teacher assessment

KEY WORDS Matching key concepts to their definitions

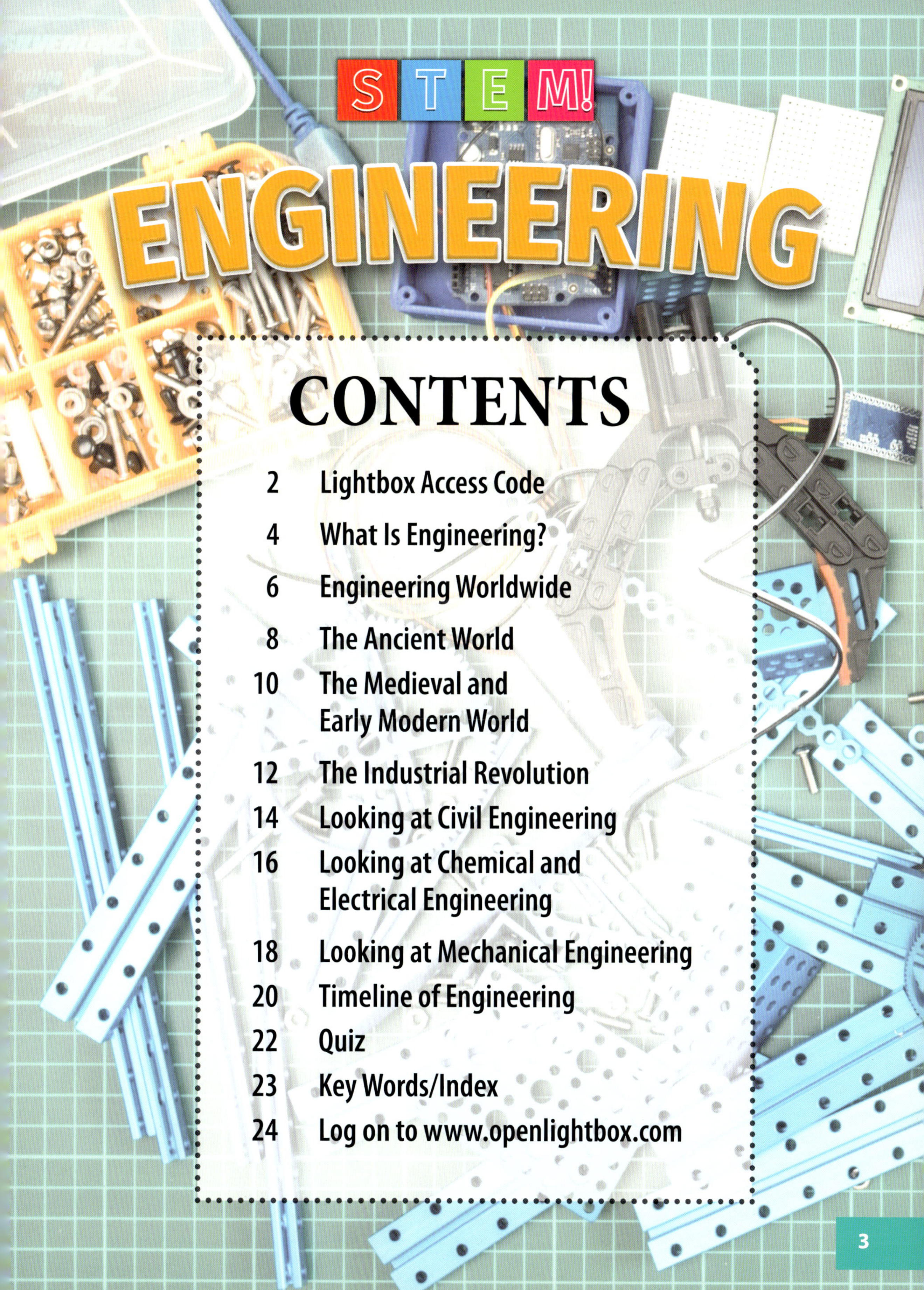

CONTENTS

WHAT IS ENGINEERING?

Engineering is the science of designing and building things. Engineers make engines and machines such as vehicles. They build structures such as bridges and roads. Engineers work with materials ranging from invisible electrical charges to slabs of stone and **concrete**. The practical science of engineering developed from basic principles of math, physics, and chemistry. It uses the latest technology available to put those principles into practice.

Different branches of engineering are all demonstrated in the automobile. In a modern car, the internal combustion engine that drives it, the electronics and computer systems that control it, the **aerodynamic** shape that gives speed and comfort, and the braking system that keeps the passengers safe are all engineered. The engine is created by **mechanical engineers**, the control systems are devised by **electrical engineers**, and the fuel is manufactured by **chemical engineers**. The road it runs on is built by **civil engineers**.

▲ Engineers built horse-drawn chariots in the ancient world using the technology of wheels linked by a shaft. They found a balance between lightness and strength.

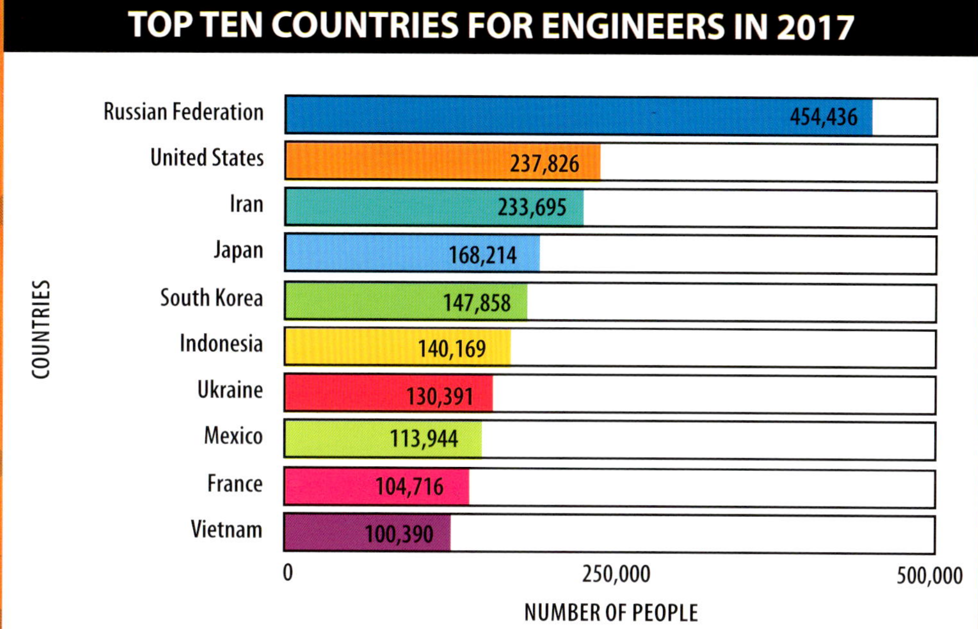

The science of physics shows how a force such as wind can affect the behavior of solid materials. Engineers have to understand how the wind will affect all the different materials that are used in the structure being made. These materials could be steel, stone, glass, or wood.

Engineers are not only theoretical scientists. They have to predict and test the answers to practical problems. What they make has to be safe and able to do the job for which it is intended. The modern world is shaped by engineering miracles that have developed from scientific research and experimentation over centuries.

▲ Racing cars are marvels of modern engineering. They have complex engines and are stable at extremely high speeds.

ENGINEERING WORLDWIDE

There were many impressive examples of engineering in the ancient world. The pyramids of ancient Egypt were a striking example of engineering skill. The ancient Romans were innovative in their use of concrete, and pioneers of road building. In ancient China, huge engineering projects were undertaken. The Great Wall of China and the Jing-Hang Grand Canal survive to this day.

The new manufacturing processes that started with the **Industrial Revolution** in Great Britain in about 1760 quickly spread across the world. Coal and iron were used for new manufacturing processes. **Steam engines** and machinery revolutionized the way people lived, with the building of factories that made **mass-production** possible. In more recent times, engineers are using their skill and technology in ways that impact almost every aspect of daily life.

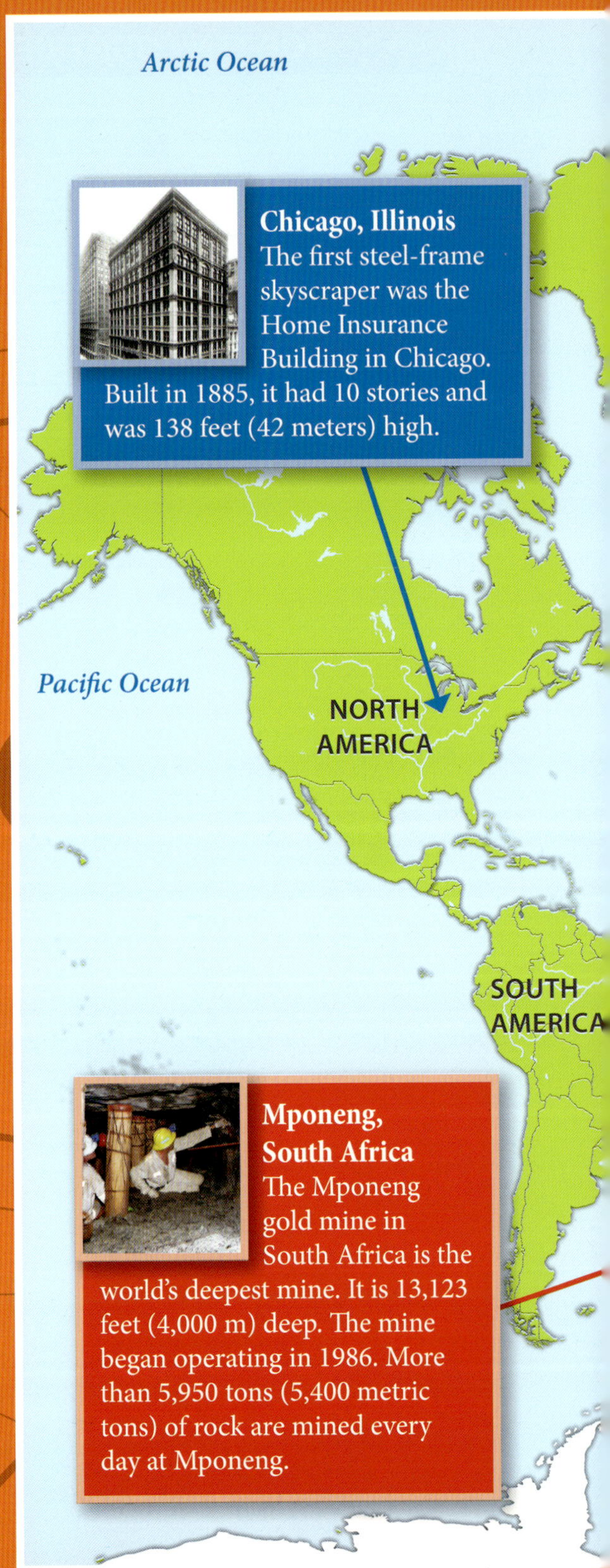

Chicago, Illinois
The first steel-frame skyscraper was the Home Insurance Building in Chicago. Built in 1885, it had 10 stories and was 138 feet (42 meters) high.

Mponeng, South Africa
The Mponeng gold mine in South Africa is the world's deepest mine. It is 13,123 feet (4,000 m) deep. The mine began operating in 1986. More than 5,950 tons (5,400 metric tons) of rock are mined every day at Mponeng.

Newcastle, Great Britain
Robert Stephenson's steam locomotive, the *Rocket,* was built in Newcastle in 1829. Its innovative design led to the development of other steam engine technology.

Rome, Italy
The Pantheon in Rome was built in the second century AD. It is a feat of engineering, given the available technology. It has the largest unreinforced concrete dome ever created.

Beijing, China
The Jing-Hang Grand Canal is the longest and probably the oldest canal in the world. Construction began in the fifth century BC. It is 1,104 miles (1,776 kilometers) long.

The Ancient World

There were three main branches of engineering in the ancient world. Engineering skills were used to construct houses and public buildings, to control water supplies, and to develop new weapons for warfare. The ancient Egyptian, Imhotep, is credited with being the first engineer. He designed the Pyramid of Djoser, one of the earliest pyramids, in the twenty-seventh century BC. Pyramid building was a real feat of engineering. The pyramid of Djoser was a **step pyramid** made from limestone blocks. Each huge stone block weighed up to 15 tons (13 metric tons). These were moved into position using rollers, ropes, and pulleys. When it was finished, the pyramid was 203 feet (62 m) high.

▲ Archimedes used his engineering skills to defend the city of Syracuse from the Romans in 214 BC. He is said to have reflected the Sun's rays off a giant mirror to set fire to enemy ships.

In ancient Mesopotamia, engineers used waterwheels to control the flow of water from the Tigris and Euphrates Rivers. They created **levees** and canals to direct water into the fields for **irrigation**. Mesopotamian engineers also developed the use of the wheel by attaching an **axle** to make carts and war chariots.

From the fourth century BC, the Romans built roads across their empire. They dug shallow trenches between drainage ditches. The trench was lined with stone slabs, and then topped with layers of sand, mortar, and large stones. Roman **aqueducts** were built to carry water from springs into the cities, where it was used in homes and public bathhouses.

The baths of Carcalla in Rome could hold **1,600 bathers** at any one time.

The Claudia aqueduct carried water **44 miles** (70 km) to Rome.

The Roman Pont du Gard aqueduct in France drops **56 feet** (17 m) over a distance of 30 miles (48 km).

Roman aqueducts often crossed deep valleys. They were built so that they sloped gently downward, to carry the flow of water from the hills.

The Medieval and Early Modern World

In the period between the end of the western Roman Empire in 476 AD and the Industrial Revolution of the 1700s, there were many developments in engineering.

In China, two major engineering projects employed thousands of laborers. One was the building of the Jing-Hang Grand Canal, linking the cities of Beijing and Huangzhou. The other was the continuation of the Great Wall of China. Successive Chinese emperors had already made additions to the Great Wall, particularly the Ming emperors of the 1400s.

Thousands of waterwheels were built throughout the medieval Islamic world. They were essential for irrigating crops.

In the Islamic world, engineers continued to develop irrigation schemes in Egypt and the Middle East. Waterwheel technology enabled irrigation to be tightly controlled, and there were said to be 5,000 waterwheels along just one river in Islamic Spain. Wind power was also harnessed to drive windmills for grinding corn.

In Europe, huge cathedrals were built from the tenth century onward. They were constructed using new techniques such as **flying buttresses** to support the weight of the structure. Engineers also built castles for defence in times of war and designed catapults and **trebuchets** that could throw huge rocks and other missiles to destroy the castle walls of enemies.

INCA ENGINEERING

When European conquerors arrived in South America in the sixteenth century, they came across people with very different engineering skills. The Incas had not invented the wheel, they did not have horses, and much of their empire was in the high mountains. Travel and communication systems were quite different from those in Europe. The Incas built grass and rope **suspension bridges** across deep ravines, and constructed narrow stone roads with steps to climb the slopes of the Andes mountains.

The Incas also had ways of cutting stones without the use of iron tools. Instead, they used stone, bronze, or copper tools. The cut stones fitted together perfectly without needing to be fixed with **cement**.

▲ Inca rope bridges in Peru were lightweight, but extremely strong.

The use of **gunpowder** from the 1300s onward greatly extended the role of engineers. They were needed to make and operate cannons. They also built defenses to resist cannonballs.

One of the greatest developments in engineering in the early modern world came in shipbuilding. By the 1500s, large wooden sailing ships with three or more masts were crossing the oceans between continents carrying heavy cargoes. They were the most advanced machines of their day.

▶ During the Ming Dynasty, the Great Wall of China was 3,889 miles (6,269 km) long.

The Industrial Revolution

The Industrial Revolution that began in Great Britain in about 1760 changed the world. It was a period that saw a change from a largely land-based farming society to one based on industry and machine manufacturing. A major advance was in the use of coal to provide energy. Burning coal gives off more heat than burning wood. When coal is heated in an air-free environment, it produces **coke**. This burns at an even higher temperature than coal. Coke made the production of iron easier and cheaper. Iron was a vital material for the development of industry.

Steel is iron mixed with carbon to make it harder. As it is harder than iron, steel makes better tools. Steel became easier to manufacture in 1856, when Henry Bessemer, a British engineer, discovered a process to create a new form of lightweight, flexible steel by blowing air across molten iron. With the development of mass-produced metals, it was possible to make metal tools such as **lathes**, screws, rivets, and pins. They could be manufactured cheaply and efficiently to any size that might be required.

The use of coal power led to the development of steam engines. Before steam power, factories and mills were largely powered by water, wind, or horse. Steam engines soon replaced the use of windmills and waterwheels.

The first bridge made entirely from cast iron still spans the River Severn in England. It was designed by Abraham Darby in 1779.

There was also a revolution in the production of chemicals. This was because large metal chambers heated by coke could now be used to heat different chemicals to create new substances. Household items such as detergents could now be mass-produced.

Electricity was also developed during the Industrial Revolution. Benjamin Franklin, one of America's Founding Fathers, experimented with electricity in the 1750s. In 1822, British scientist Michael Faraday demonstrated electricity generation. The first department of electrical engineering was set up in the United States in 1886.

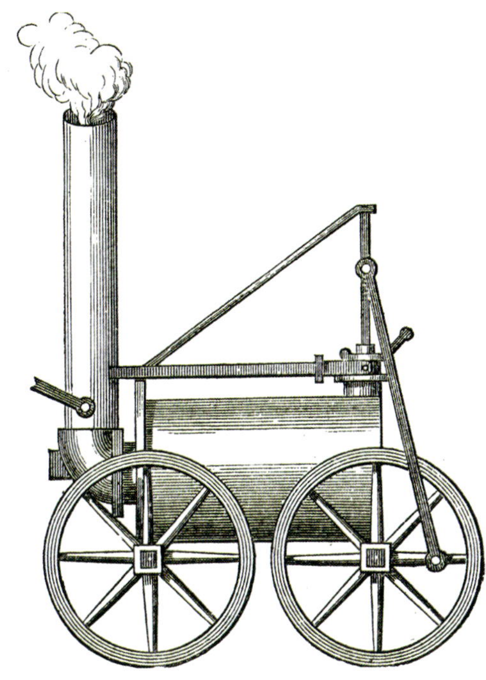

Richard Trevithick's 1808 locomotive, nicknamed "Catch Me Who Can," was one of the first steam locomotives to run on a specially built track.

JOHN SMEATON

John Smeaton (1724–1792) was the first person to call himself a "civil engineer." By 1759, he had become an expert in windmills and watermills and was commissioned to design and build a lighthouse. The challenge was to build its foundations under water. To solve the problem, he had to work out how to make a type of cement that would set hard under water. He heated limestone using coke. This cement formed the basis of concrete. Concrete had been known to the Romans, but had fallen into disuse. Smeaton's rediscovery of concrete revolutionized construction methods.

Smeaton's Eddystone lighthouse was rebuilt on land in England in 1877.

Looking at Civil Engineering

Civil engineers are involved in the design and building of large constructions, including houses, roads, bridges, canals, dams, airports, sewers, railways, schools, and other public buildings. The first degree in civil engineering in the United States was awarded in 1835. A degree in civil engineering covers physics, math, and specific engineering topics such as knowledge of materials and how they behave, and site management. It can take more than eight years to qualify as a civil engineer. About 46,000 civil engineers graduate yearly from colleges in the United States.

▲ The Burj Khalifa in Dubai is the tallest building in the world, at 2,717 feet (828 m).

There are many specializations within the science of civil engineering. One that has become important in the modern world is environmental engineering, in which the treatment of waste products and issues such as water purification are important. These are now vital considerations in all large civil engineering projects.

In places such as Japan and California, where earthquakes are commonplace, civil engineers have developed earthquake-proof buildings. Coastal engineering is also increasingly important, as the rise in sea levels threaten some of the world's most populated regions.

Big civil engineering projects catch the public imagination. As technology improves, engineers design taller buildings, bigger dams, longer bridges, and deeper tunnels. A big project may employ thousands of engineers, all with different specializations.

The Danyang-Kunshan Grand Bridge in China spans **102.4 miles** (165 km).

The Burj Khalifa opened on **January 4, 2010**.

The Three Gorges Dam in China cost **30 billion** U.S. dollars to build.

The building of the Three Gorges Dam in China caused concern among environmentalists. They were worried about the damage it was doing to the landscape and wildlife in the area.

Looking at Chemical and Electrical Engineering

Chemical engineering involves many branches of technology. It also involves principles of chemistry, physics, math, biology, and economics. Chemical engineers design chemical plants or industrial factories that manufacture, process, or convert sometimes dangerous chemicals and other raw materials on a large scale. The plants produce consumer products such as soaps, detergents, cosmetics, plastics, pesticides, food additives, and numerous other products.

The American Institute of Chemical Engineers (AIChemE) was founded in 1908. For much of the early 1900s, chemical engineers were engaged in the discovery, drilling, and refining of oil and gas. By the mid-1900s, the manufacture of plastics was a major part of the chemical industry.

▲ Chemical plants are complex structures. When designing a chemical plant, engineers take into account the safety of the workers and the effects the plant will have on the environment.

Electrical engineering is a branch of engineering that deals with the technology of electricity. It was first recognized as a profession in the late 1800s, after the invention of the electric telegraph. Early pioneers of electrical engineering include Thomas Edison, who invented the electric light bulb in 1879, and Guglielmo Marconi, who invented the radio in 1896.

In the 1950s, new technologies such as transistors, integrated circuits, and microelectronics enabled engineers to design electronic systems that control machines. Today's electrical engineers design devices from electric power plants to tiny microprocessors that are used in computers, cell phones, and computers. Computer-aided design (CAD) systems are used by electrical engineers to test how electrical devices and systems might work. CAD systems are used to model national power grids, air traffic control, telecommunications systems, and much more.

The importance of electrical engineering is set to increase. Fossil fuel power plants release pollution and harm the environment. The production of clean electric power is a priority for people in the 2000s.

▲ Electrical engineering became more complex after small components such as transistors were invented in the 1950s.

THE BHOPAL DISASTER

Chemical engineering can be dangerous. The importance of safety in chemical engineering plants was demonstrated by the Bhopal disaster in India. In 1984, 3,787 people died after an explosion at the Union Carbide pesticide plant in Bhopal. The plant had been making a pesticide using methyl isocyanate. This chemical was stored as a liquid. When water got into a tank containing this liquid, it reacted with the water to form a gas that exploded. The gas cloud covered the town of Bhopal. As well as the people who died, 170,000 other people were treated for the effects of inhaling the gas.

Looking at Mechanical Engineering

Mechanical engineers make and look after machines, from office chairs to gearboxes, and from ships to space stations. Mechanical engineering overlaps with many other branches of engineering. It has a long history in industry, and before the Industrial Revolution, played an important role in the development of weapons and vehicles for use in warfare. More recently, it has become connected to biotechnology. This is the design of machines that help the human body work more efficiently.

In the 1600s, the Dutch scientist, Christiaan Huygens, published major works on the study of mechanics. He invented the pendulum clock and other timekeeping devices. The parts needed for a clock, and the tools to make the parts, were handmade and expensive. The Industrial Revolution changed that. Precisely machined metal parts became easy to mass-produce, and the machine age had begun.

▲ The cogs and wheels inside a clock or watch are made from different metals. Each part is finely machined for accuracy.

Mechanical engineering skills range from a basic understanding of scientific principles to practical knowledge of materials and how they behave. There are three essential areas of mechanical engineering. One is mechanics, or the study of how forces produce motion. Another is **structural analysis**, the study of the effects of loads on physical structures. The third is **thermodynamics**, the study of how energy, particularly heat, works within a machine.

Aerospace engineering is a major specialization within mechanical engineering. Aerospace engineers design airplanes, space shuttles, satellites, and missiles. They develop new technologies, and might specialize in commercial aircraft, military fighter jets, or helicopters. Aerospace engineers are experts in the principles of aerodynamics and thermodynamics.

It takes four years to train as an entry-level mechanical engineer. A master's degree takes another two to four years. A PhD will take a further seven years to complete.

A Boeing 747 airplane has more than **SIX MILLION** separate parts.

Spacecraft have to be able to withstand **temperatures** of more **3,000 Fahrenheit** (1,649 Centigrade).

The North American **X-15 aircraft** can fly at speeds of **4,474 miles per hour** (7,200 km/h).

Aerospace engineers design and build jet engines. A jet engine burns fuel with air in a chemical reaction called combustion. This makes enough energy to power the jet plane.

TIMELINE OF ENGINEERING

Engineering has been part of human society since civilization began. People applied simple engineering methods to building shelters, farming, and warfare. Problem solving is common to all branches of engineering. Today, the main function of engineering is to research, develop, design, build, and operate all types of constructions and devices for the benefit of humankind. The results of such endeavors, ancient and modern, have shaped the modern world.

2560 BC | 500 AD | 1000 AD | 1600 | 1650

312 BC
Roman engineers build the Appian Way, Rome's first large-scale stone and gravel road.

2560 BC
Ancient Egyptians build the Great Pyramid, which still stands. For centuries, it was the world's largest building.

1045 AD
Chinese engineers develop the first gunpowder weapons.

1656
Christiaan Huygens invents the pendulum clock, the most accurate timepiece to date.

1781
The world's first bridge made from iron is built in Great Britain.

1856
Henry Bessemer's first steel manufacturing factory is opened.

1931
The Empire State Building is completed in New York City.

1700 | 1800 | 1900 | 1950 | 2019

1759
John Smeaton designs the Eddystone lighthouse using cement and concrete.

2005
The world's largest airliner, the Airbus 380, makes its first flight. It can carry more than 800 passengers.

2019
There are more than 1.6 million engineers of all types working in the United States.

QUIZ

ONE
Who is credited as being the first known engineer?

TWO
What did engineers in ancient Mesopotamia use waterwheels for?

THREE
What did Roman aqueducts carry?

FOUR
What structure runs from Beijing to Huangzhou?

FIVE
What is the function of a flying buttress?

SIX
What did John Smeaton rediscover in the 1700s?

SEVEN
What are thermodynamics?

EIGHT
What is AIChemE?

TEN
What is CAD?

NINE
Where is the Three Gorges Dam?

ANSWERS

ONE Imhotep **TWO** To control the flow of water from the Tigris and Euphrates Rivers **THREE** Water **FOUR** The Jing-Hang Grand Canal **FIVE** To support the weight of a structure **SIX** How to make waterproof cement and concrete **SEVEN** The study of how heat works within a machine **EIGHT** The American Institute of Chemical Engineers **NINE** China **TEN** Computer-Aided Design

KEY WORDS

aerodynamic: a shape that passes through the air easily

aerospace engineering: maintaining aircraft and their engines

aqueducts: long structures for transporting water

axle: the pole that connects a pair of wheels

cement: a powder that mixes with water to bind minerals

chemical engineers: engineers who use chemicals

civil engineers: engineers who build and maintain roads, buildings, dams, and other structures

coke: coal that has been heated in special ovens.

concrete: cement mixed with gravel or sand

electrical engineers: engineers who maintain electrical systems

flying buttresses: supports for walls to allow them to carry more weight

gunpowder: an explosive substance used in warfare

Industrial Revolution: changes in technology and production during the 1700s

irrigation: controlling water to help crops grow

lathes: machines for shaping wood or metal

levees: barriers designed to stop flooding

mass-production: making many identical items

mechanical engineers: engineers who use and maintain tools and engines

steam engines: engines driven by steam power

step pyramid: a pyramid with stepped blocks up the sides

structural analysis: the study of how loads affect structures

suspension bridges: bridges that are suspended and supported from above

thermodynamics: the study of how heat works in a system

trebuchets: machines used in medieval siege warfare for hurling stones or other missiles

INDEX

LIGHTBOX

SUPPLEMENTARY RESOURCES

Click on the plus icon found in the bottom left corner of each spread to open additional teacher resources.

- Download and print the book's quizzes and activities
- Access curriculum correlations
- Explore additional web applications that enhance the Lightbox experience

LIGHTBOX DIGITAL TITLES
Packed full of integrated media

VIDEOS

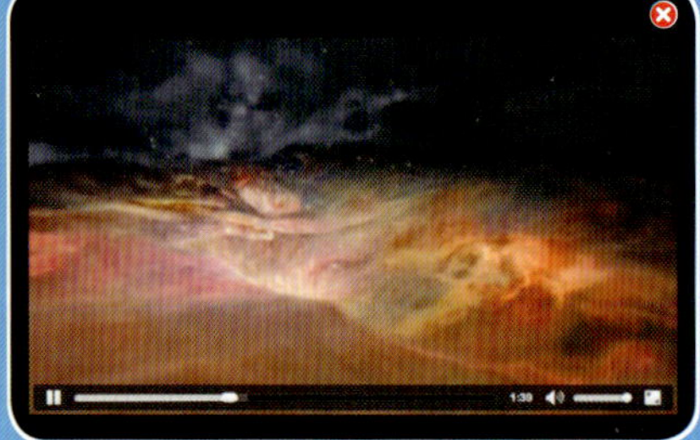

INTERACTIVE MAPS

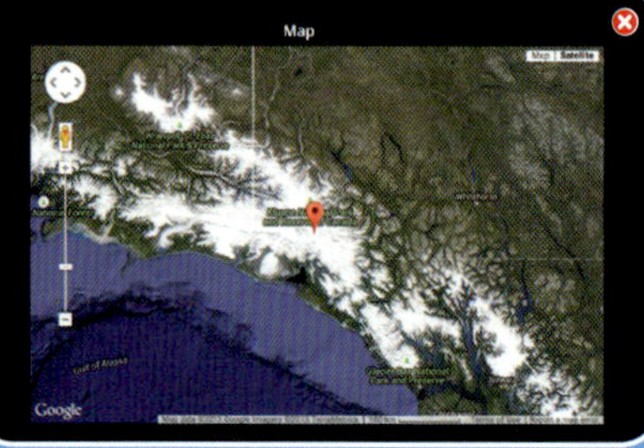

WEBLINKS

SLIDESHOWS

QUIZZES

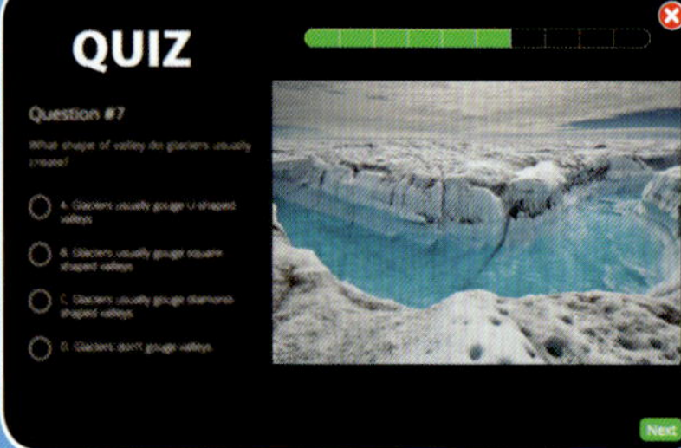

OPTIMIZED FOR
- ✓ TABLETS
- ✓ WHITEBOARDS
- ✓ COMPUTERS
- ✓ AND MUCH MORE!

Published by Smartbook Media Inc.
350 5th Avenue, 59th Floor New York, NY 10118
Website: www.openlightbox.com

Project Coordinator: Heather Kissock
Art Director: Terry Paulhus

Library of Congress Control Number: 2019942198

ISBN 978-1-5105-4416-1 (hardcover)
ISBN 978-1-5105-4417-8 (multi-user eBook)

Printed in Guangzhou, China
1 2 3 4 5 6 7 8 9 0 23 22 21 20 19

072019
121819

Photo Credits
Every reasonable effort has been made to trace ownership and to obtain permission to reprint copyright material. The publisher would be pleased to have any errors or omissions brought to its attention so that they may be corrected in subsequent printings.

The publisher acknowledges Getty Images, Alamy, and Shutterstock as its primary image suppliers for this title.